Kiwi

Jenny Jones
Photographs by Rod Morris

REED

CONTENTS

INTRODUCTION

New Zealand has never had a huge diversity of species within its flora and fauna. Some orders are represented by just one genus, and several genera have one or two species. For example, frogs are the only order of amphibians in New Zealand, and among land mammals present at the time of human occupation there were only three species of bat.

However, what early New Zealand lacked in species variety, it made up for in the rich endemic nature of those species.

New Zealand had an environment that was not dominated by large numbers of mammals, that is, the large browsing and predatory animals found in other countries. New Zealand did have many birds, none more extraordinary than the kiwi.

The kiwi is endemic to New Zealand and includes some unique species of birds. They are one of the oldest surviving families of birds to be found in New Zealand.

Since human colonisation of New Zealand there has been no other animal that has fascinated and caused as much curiosity as the kiwi. The kiwi's origins and lineage have been a matter of discussion throughout the scientific world.

Recent DNA work shows that the kiwi are more closely related to the cassowary and the emu than they are to moa. There are various kiwi forms divided into two distinct groups: the brown kiwi and the spotted kiwi. There are two species in each group: the North Island brown and the southern tokoeka, and the little spotted and great spotted kiwis respectively. There are two varieties of North Island brown kiwi: the North Island brown and the Okarito brown kiwi, and two varieties of the southern tokoeka: the Fiordland/Stewart Island tokoeka and the Haast tokoeka.

Prehistoric distribution

If you were asked to imagine a wild place where kiwi lived millions of years ago, what would you give as an answer? Thick forest or bush? Imagine sub-zero temperatures with snow and ice and kiwi foraging in and around tussocks for invertebrates to eat. Doesn't sound right? Picture kiwi living between 800 and 1000 metres above sea level in ice-clad glacier landscapes, moving about with the skill of a mountaineer.

No? Well, this was where and how the great spotted kiwi, the largest of the kiwi species, lived. They were as sure-footed as a mountain goat.

Before human visits and subsequent colonisation, New Zealand was covered in dense forest, extensive swamps and wetlands, high tussocklands and alpine habitat. The kiwi were not dependent on any specific environment. They had to compete with such species as weka and snipe and share their environment with all other New Zealand species.

Kiwi were present in all habitats throughout the North, South and Stewart islands, as well as on many of the smaller islands, such as Kapiti Island, Little and Great Barrier islands and D'urville Island.

Palaeontologists have found kiwi fossil bones throughout New Zealand, in places from sand dunes to subalpine zones and all habitats in-between. From these bones scientists have been able to establish how widespread each of the various species was and where most birds were throughout time.

5

Kiwi — our bird

Class: Aves
Order: Apterygiformes
Suborder: Apteryges
Family: Apterygidae

The kiwi's scientific name, *Apteryx*, is from the Greek word *apterugos*, which means 'without wings'. The kiwi was first named by Shaw and Nodder in 1813.

The origins of the kiwi are lost in time but present scientific thought is that they came to New Zealand when the land mass that was to become Australia was still close to New Zealand. One evolutionary line of primitive birds gave rise to the group known as ratites. This group contains kiwi, ostrich, rhea, cassowary, emu and all the now extinct moa and elephant birds. The word ratite is from the Latin word *ratis*, which describes a flat breastbone with no

Kiwi — a bird like no other

Kiwi are animals with a backbone and feathers. This makes them definitely birds. But they are like no other bird as they are 'K-selected' species, that is they are long-lived, slow breeders and population numbers will increase to fill up a habitat.

In addition to being the smallest of the flightless ratites, the kiwi has the most uncharacteristic morphology (external features). These are quite different from all other ratites, not to mention all other birds.

keel (this is the piece of bone that sticks out of the middle of the breastbone; think of the pointy piece that you see on the breastbone of a chicken's skeleton). This flat breastbone is a feature of some of the ratite birds because they are flightless and no longer have the requirement of the sharper V-shaped breastbone that is necessary for muscle attachment in birds that fly. There is one member of the ratite group that does fly — the tinamou.

Kiwi are descended from a Gondwanan ancestor that flew. Just how and when the kiwi's ancestors arrived in New Zealand has been cause for much speculation. Kiwi did come out of the mists of time, but did they walk or did they fly?

Kiwi skeletons reveal their story. The oldest kiwi fossil bones found date to about one million years old. However, they give no hint of what the kiwi's ancestors looked like. Today's kiwi still has wing bones and 'leftover' wings, which indicates that the kiwi's ancestors flew.

Too weird to be a bird?

In the 1800s the kiwi's existence was thought to be nothing more than a figment of early explorers' imaginations. So much so that when the first kiwi skin, with head and feet attached, was sent to Britain in 1812, people questioned whether or not it was really the skin of a bird. The kiwi was seen as a curiosity and a freak throughout the scientific world of the day.

The skin arrived into the hands of George Shaw, an assistant keeper at the British Museum. It was not catalogued into the museum but was kept by Shaw in his private collection.

At first the skin was wrongly identified as a penguin. The first published illustrations of a kiwi show a penguin-like bird in an open, sparsely vegetated environment. Despite this error, illustrations of the feathers, feet and the beak were anatomically accurate. Shaw eventually reclassified the kiwi as a ratite bird in 1913, naming it *Apteryx australis*. After his death, Shaw's estate was auctioned and the kiwi skin was bought and kept by the thirteenth earl of Derby. The well-travelled, poorly labelled kiwi skin remained in the Earl's family until it was passed to the Liverpool Museum in England, where it remains today.

In 1835 the skin of a North Island kiwi reached ornithologists in London. Following this many kiwi and information about them appeared in reports, and when enough specimens had been received at the Zoological Society in London some were sent to other parts of Europe and America.

Much interest in this peculiar bird followed, with many visits to New Zealand by naturalists and zoologists to study kiwi and see them live in their natural habitat.

What's in a name? Plenty, if it's 'Kiwi'!

New Zealanders are proud to be called Kiwis. Think about how often you hear news headlines like 'Kiwi wins again', or 'missing Kiwi found safe and well'. We instantly know the news is about a New Zealander.

New Zealand is one of the only countries in the world to have such an engrained link to one of its natural species, a link that is part of everyday life.

There are numerous products that carry the Kiwi name and a picture of the bird, its familiar head-down stance immediately identifying the item as being from or about New Zealand. We see it on products such as bacon, shoe polish and even on two of our coins. The Kiwi flag is proudly waved by fans at sporting and cultural events. We have even coined the word 'kiwiana', which refers to any objects or items that reflect New Zealand culture.

Maori and the kiwi

Maori held kiwi in the highest esteem. The kiwi are included in their mythology and lore where its mystique and curiosity are woven into wonderful stories.

Tane Mahuta, the god of the forest, created his world by separating his parents, Ranginui (the Sky Father) and Papatuanuku (the Earth Mother). In so doing his world of the trees and animals was created. Kiwi was the most precious of all the birds. To help protect kiwi Tane placed him in the dark shadows, close to his Earth Mother so she could nurture him.

Another myth has it that during a time when Tane was battling a plague of insects in his forest the kiwi was the only bird prepared to help him. However, the price for coming to the ground was that he lost his brightly coloured plumage to become 'as dark as the shadows'.

For early Maori, there was great ceremony and ritual to be observed when hunting kiwi. A powerful karakia (chant) was performed to ensure a good hunt and also to give thanks to Tane Mahuta. Kiwi were hunted at night, using kuri (dogs) and smouldering torches. When startled by the kuri or torchlight the kiwi would freeze, pushing its bill into the ground in an attempt to avoid detection.

Kiwi were carefully prepared for eating. The feathers were plucked and stored for later use in a woven cloak. Sometimes the skins were also used for cloaks. The feather cloaks, kahu kiwi, were highly prized and were a taonga (treasure), only worn by those of high rank. Some kiwi were preserved in their fat and placed in containers made of totara bark. These were then stored for later use. Kiwi leg bones were used to make musical instruments such as the nose flute.

Kiwi are also part of Maori proverb, for example a person arriving after dark or a stranger coming to the home who stands in the darkness is said to be 'manu huna a Tane' — the hidden bird of Tane, just like a kiwi.

Diggeress Te Kanawa with a kahu kiwi made from the feathers of a North Island brown kiwi.

What makes a kiwi a kiwi?

Kiwi stand up to 45 centimetres in height and females are larger than the males. The females are 10–20 percent heavier than the males and can weigh between 3 and 5 kilograms. They average about the size of a rugby ball. Different species are different sizes — the little spotted kiwi is the smallest kiwi and is smaller than a rugby ball while the great spotted kiwi is twice the size.

Kiwi have a very reduced upper body bone structure. They have no keel on their breastbone and no pectoral muscles. Compared to other birds, they have exceedingly broad and strong ribs. This could be because they do not have wings that protect the chest region of the body.

Southern tokoeka.

The head
The skull and windpipe
The kiwi has a big skull (the skull includes the beak), with a small brain and a long, looped neck that is usually held forward. Like all birds, kiwi have rings of bone surrounding the windpipe (trachea) called tracheal rings. There are at least 100 of these rings.

Subfossil of skull of great spotted kiwi.

Sight
Kiwi are mostly nocturnal and have adapted to moving around in the dark in very dense undergrowth. However, kiwi on Stewart Island will quite happily come out during the day!

Nocturnal animals usually have very large eyes and highly developed sight, but not the kiwi. Kiwi have small, black and beady eyes. In fact, scientists have found that their eye structure is unique and is unlike that of any other bird. Kiwi are not blind and their eyesight is not

11

as poor as has previously been thought. The sight they do have is enough for their needs and suits a kiwi very well. To compensate for their 'lesser' sight, kiwi have very well developed senses of touch and smell.

Southern tokoeka probing for sandhoppers.

Ears
Kiwi have large, visible earholes. They have a very acute sense of hearing. They will often reply to each other's calls from more than 200 metres and on very still nights up to as far as 450 metres apart.

Voice
The kiwi is a very vocal bird and has a range of calls that it only gives at night. Different species have different calls; as do males and females of the same species. Calls are used as communication. There are breeding calls, territorial calls and 'keeping in touch with a mate' calls, which can be loud if kiwi are apart, or soft and comforting if they are together.

Calling depends on the weather. During periods of a full moon or strong winds kiwi call less frequently. Males tend to call more than females, especially during the breeding season as they are trying to attract a mate. Calls are often more frequent in the hours following dusk and carry through the forest for some 200 metres or more. Duets are not uncommon between a bonded pair of kiwi.

Kiwi hold their heads with their bills up to call. The brown kiwi does a fast bow of the head and bill between calls. Young kiwi do not call until at least a year old and their call is immature. As they grow older they gain confidence and a strong voice that is used to compete with their elders. When threatened, kiwi hiss and clap their bill.

It is thought the name 'kiwi' came from its call. Certainly male brown kiwi sound like they are saying 'kee wee' but this sound is not easily heard when listening to other species of kiwi.

The bill
A kiwi's bill is a perfect tool for the detection of food. The bill, which is unique to kiwi, is up to 200 millimetres long. There are two small nostrils at the tip of the bill instead of at the base, as in all other birds. The upper mandible (the top bill) is slightly longer and more rounded, curving over the lower mandible.

Towards the base of the bill kiwi have a valve that stops dirt and water going into their lungs. They clear dirt and water in their bill by sucking their breath in through the open bill and snorting it out through the nostrils, making a loud snuffling sound. This same valve allows kiwi to feed in wet areas such as rivers and streams.

Kiwi do not have teeth but they do have a very rough, pointy pink tongue to assist in the swallowing of food.

Kiwi have a number of long bristles at the base of the bill, which are highly modified feathers. These look like the whiskers we see on a cat or a dog. Like a cat or a dog, kiwi use their whiskers to feel what is around them. These whiskers also help to protect their eyes.

A kiwi's sense of smell is highly developed. Food can be detected more than 50 millimetres below ground. They vigorously probe their bill into the soil, often getting their whole bill below ground. They will also sniff the air to determine what is in their surroundings.

The region of the brain concerned with the kiwi's sense of smell is highly developed and extremely functional. In the bird world the kiwi's very developed senses are matched only by a few seabirds such as the snowy petrel and some vultures.

Whiskers on a North Island brown kiwi.

Bill tip and nostrils of North Island brown kiwi.

North Island brown kiwi probing for food.

 13

The body
Wings
Although a kiwi's wings are small, they contain the same bones as those found in birds that can fly. The wing is about 2.5 centimetres long. It has very few feathers and there is a claw at the end. The wing remains invisible, beneath the kiwi's plumage. There are usually 'bill grooves' in feathers that cover the body underneath the wing, which show that the kiwi sleeps with its bill under its wing. Some birds choose one wing to put their bill under, some use both.

A bird's flight muscles are normally well developed, and constitute a large proportion of its body mass and are costly in terms of energy. For the kiwi, as in other flightless birds, this is not the case as they do not fly. They can put their energy to better use.

The wing of a kiwi is very small.

The tail
Kiwi do not have the specialised tail bones that birds of flight have. Instead, their tail vertebrae have fused into a small lump. This is one of the features that gives the kiwi its distinctive pear shape.

Feathers and camouflage
The feathers of the kiwi are simple in structure, without the barbules that lock the rami together in birds that fly. This gives kiwi a scruffy, shaggy appearance. Their feathers look more like hair than feathers and when stroked, they feel harsh and prickly. There is no difference between the plumage of males and females. Kiwi have a lower body temperature than all other birds. At about 38 degrees Celsius a kiwi's body temperature is very close to that of humans.

In contrast to flighted birds that moult at the same time every year, kiwi moult throughout the year. Feathers constantly fall out as the kiwi brushes against the sides of its burrow or it squeezes through gaps, so they are always being renewed. The plumage of the kiwi can be brown, dappled grey, black, rufous-red or white.

When a kiwi becomes stressed it freezes. Looking from above, its body shape, the texture of its plumage and its colour melt the kiwi into forest vegetation. In prehistoric times this camouflage was the kiwi's best defence when natural predators were other birds like the laughing owl, Eyles's harrier, the falcon and Haast's eagle. These were all birds that hunted

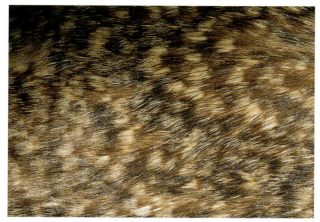

Feathers of great spotted kiwi.

Feathers of North Island brown kiwi.

Feathers of little spotted kiwi.

from above. The laughing owl was the main nocturnal predator of the four and could easily take a chick or small adult. The laughing owl is thought to have hunted more by sound than sight so the kiwi's colours were of little use.

Eyles's harrier, three times heavier than the present Australian harrier, and Haast's eagle, the largest eagle to ever have lived, both hunted by day and dusk. As on Stewart Island, the kiwi may have come out during the daytime and they certainly would have been active at dusk in other parts of New Zealand. If the kiwi was not sleeping in its burrow, it would nestle into vegetation with its bill under its wing to resemble a lump of rotting log to avoid detection.

White female North Island brown kiwi. The colouring of this bird is rare.

15

Legs and feet

As well as having plumage that gives excellent camouflage and therefore protection from predators, kiwi have extremely strong feet and legs and their claws are lethal weapons.

A kiwi's stocky legs make up one-third of its total body weight. Unlike a bird that flies whose bones have a honeycomb appearance, the kiwi's bones contain marrow and they are very strong.

The feet are also strong and the claws are curved and razor-sharp. There are three front-facing toes. The centre claw is the longest and there is a short back claw. This enables the kiwi to run very fast and it can travel for an extended period of time over long distances, sometimes as far as up to 15 kilometres in a night.

Feet of North Island brown kiwi showing the claws and padded foot.

TERRITORY AND BURROWS

Kiwi usually occupy their territory in pairs. Their home ground can be as large as 60 football fields. Both males and females defend their territory, which can include all types of landform and terrain. Tough, callused pads on the soles of a kiwi's feet and its crampon-like claws makes it very surefooted.

Within their territory kiwi can have many burrows. They dig their burrows by using their strong legs, feet and claws and do this at spectacular speed. The kiwi moves its head out of the way and goes full speed, soil flying in all directions. The single-entrance burrows, some as long as up to 3 metres, have entrances that are just large enough for the kiwi to squeeze through. The burrows are warm and dark and the inner chamber is large enough for two kiwi to snuggle up together. Some pairs don't sleep together as each may prefer its own sleeping quarters.

Kiwi also rest and roost in holes that are not as elaborate as the ones they dig out. This may be under a tree root or in a clump of fern or other dense vegetation, or they might surround themselves with leaf litter.

A kiwi on night patrol will feed, rest and survey its territory and regularly move from burrow to burrow. Kiwi leave strong-smelling faecal material as a marker, as well as having their own sweet musky odour that also lingers. Both scents act as deterrents to other kiwi, who are led to think the owner of the territory is in residence.

A kiwi will ferociously defend its territory to the death. This can be the case when two rival males contest a territorial boundary. They may strike with one or both legs, jumping and lashing out the strong curved claws that are extended in sustained attacking and fighting situations. They also use their bill to hold their opponent down.

Top: Female North Island brown kiwi roosting in her burrow.
Right: North Island brown kiwi asleep in its day roost.

17

FOOD

Kiwi eat a variety of foods, from invertebrates found in leaf litter or under the ground to seashore sandhoppers. They also eat small freshwater crayfish and caddisfly larvae found in streams, as well as fruits and berries of such plants as the coprosma.

Food sources are dependent on where the kiwi lives. All kiwi include a large percentage of ground-dwelling animals in their diet.

Kiwi capture live food using their long bill, which they probe into the ground, smelling out the invertebrates buried below. Earthworms make up the largest percentage of the kiwi diet. A kiwi will pull a worm out of the ground using a slow stop-start method. This is to avoid breaking the worm!

Other invertebrates eaten by kiwi include moths, cicadas, flies and larvae of beetles such as the carabid beetle. They also eat spiders, centipedes, slaters, millipedes, weta and adult beetles.

MATES, EGGS AND BABIES

Mates

Male and female kiwi can bond for life. Kiwi are a long-lived species, some birds living up to 40 years. Breeding is not an annual occurrence, as kiwi have evolved a breeding pattern that results in a slow but steady population growth.

In the stable and predictable environment offered in New Zealand in prehistoric times, kiwi built their population to capacity, and as they were long-lived they only needed to breed every couple of years.

Sizes of each sex can overlap and a pair can look much the same when compared, which means that size is not helpful when determining the sex of a kiwi. On closer inspection an adult male can be distinguished from an adult female by the visible sexual organs. The male kiwi is one of a few birds that have a copulating organ (a penis).

Eggs

A male kiwi will initiate the mating process, which takes place in the burrow, by gently stroking the female on the back of her neck. After fertilisation the egg takes about two weeks before it becomes shelled and is laid. A female with egg will add an additional 20–25 percent more weight to her body. Scientists have observed that a female will stand in water when with egg, presumably to relieve her extended belly or her aching legs.

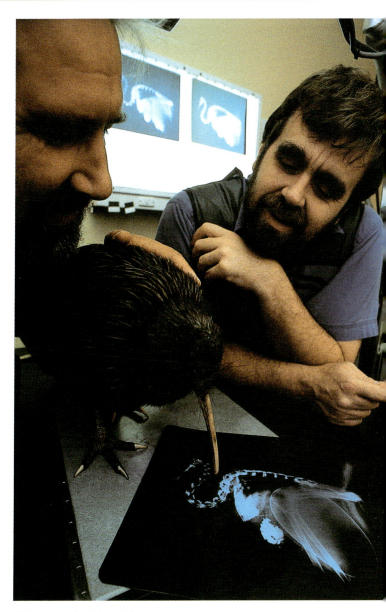

This North Island brown kiwi has just been X-rayed so her carers can see her egg.

Female kiwi have the distinction of developing the largest egg for body size of any bird, living or extinct. Kiwi are not a large bird, ranging in size from a hen to a turkey, yet the female develops, carries and produces eggs that are 20 percent of her total body weight. Compared to other ratites this ratio is considered spectacular.

Why are their eggs so big? There are two views about this. One theory is that the kiwi was once a much larger bird. Evolutionary change meant the bird got smaller but its egg did not. The other train of thought is that evolution has led to an egg that produces large, highly developed and independent offspring that need little parental care when hatched.

During the days prior to laying, the female will not feed. The female kiwi uses stored reserves of body fat to form her egg. The yolk of her egg makes up about 60 percent of the total size of the egg — compare this to many other birds' eggs, which contain only 20 percent yolk.

Eggs are slightly elliptical (one end is more pointed than the other) and all eggs vary in shape. The shell is smooth and white or has a slight greenish tinge. The egg weighs about 450 grams, about the equivalent of six hen's eggs. In all species except the brown kiwi, only one egg is laid. When the brown kiwi lays a second egg it usually does so three to four weeks after the first.

Male brown kiwi and male little spotted kiwi take responsibility for incubating their eggs. Female great spotted kiwis will help, incubating for around six hours of a 24-hour period. On average incubation takes about 75 days (10–11 weeks). The male loses a lot of body weight during incubation, as much as one-third of his total weight. He does not leave the nest, turning the eggs every day with his bill. He develops a 'brood patch' on his breast, caused by the egg constantly sitting against his body.

A kiwi in its burrow with its egg.

Babies

Kiwi chicks do not develop an 'egg tooth' like other birds. Without this small hard piece on its bill to help the chick out of its shell, it must use its legs to kick its way out. It can take up to four days for a kiwi chick to emerge. It gets no help from its parents. On hatching, the chick is a fully feathered replica of Mum and Dad.

The kiwi chick does not eat for the first seven or eight days of its life. It does not try to stand, preferring a squatting position. From seven days old the chick can stand but it does not start to forage for food. During this period the

A North Island brown kiwi chick hatching out of its egg.

A nine-day old chick catching worms.

kiwi chick is nourished by the huge yolk sac it has absorbed from its egg. This can be seen in its belly. From about a week old the chick is on its own and fends for itself. It instinctively knows how to forage for food and to take grit into its stomach to help digestion.

Parents will tolerate chicks in their territory until they are about one year old. At this stage they are forced to move on and find their own territory. Up until the kiwi is five to six years old, the species are monomorphic (the same). After this age the females become larger and heavier and develop a longer bill.

A young chick foraging.

A recently-hatched chick cuddles beneath one of its parents.

North Island brown kiwi
Apteryx mantelli

Some North Island brown kiwi grow very large, even larger than the great spotted kiwi. Juveniles are fully grown at 18–20 months of age. The average weight of an adult female is 2.5 kg and 2 kg for an adult male. The average height is 40 cm. The average length of its bill if slightly curved is 132 mm; if straight 100 mm.

The North Island brown kiwi has dark brown to reddish plumage with brown-black streaky markings running lengthwise. Its plumage is shaggy and hair-like and is harsh to the touch.

Once widespread throughout the North Island, the North Island brown kiwi today is only found in small areas of Northland, around Waikaremoana in the Ureweras, the central Hawke's Bay and around Mt Ruapehu and Taranaki. It is also on Little Barrier Island.

The North Island brown kiwi has adapted to a changing environment in the north that includes areas of farmland, scrubland and pine forests.

Okarito brown kiwi
Apteryx sp.

The Okarito brown kiwi is identified as a distinct form and is thought to be a close relative of the North Island brown kiwi.

The average weight of an adult female is 2.7 kg and less than 2 kg for an adult male. They are about 38 cm in height, making them smaller than the North Island brown kiwi.

The Okariko brown kiwi has slightly grey plumage. Its plumage is shaggy and hair-like and is harsh to the touch.

The female can lay between one and three eggs in the breeding season, which is from June to February. Incubation is shared by the male and the female. The chicks can remain with the parents for some months after hatching.

It is not known how widespread the Okarito brown kiwi once was. The present population survives in the very dense lowland forest of the Westland/Tai Poutini National Park. Their survival has been significantly assisted by the captive breeding programme called Operation Nest Egg. Their current population number is thought to be around 170.

Southern tokoeka
Apteryx australis

This kiwi is found in the South Island and on Stewart Island. On average this kiwi is larger than the North Island brown kiwi, but this figure is based on a very small amount of data and may be incorrect.

The tokoeka was once widespread throughout the South Island. Today there are a few small and isolated areas with populations from Fiordland to western Southland. They are still common on Stewart Island.

The southern tokoeka was the first brown kiwi described and the North Island brown kiwi is often considered to be a subspecies of it.

The kiwi on Stewart Island are on average larger than those in Fiordland. They have an average height of 45 cm. Their average weights are 3.3 kg for female birds and 2.5 kg for males.

The plumage of the southern tokoeka is a grey-brown or brown colour and is not as harsh to the touch as that of the North Island brown kiwi. The average bill length of the females is 120 mm and the males 100 mm.

The female lays a single egg and assists the male with incubation. The young can remain in the parents' territory for up to two years, and have been known to also assist with incubation.

It is not uncommon for the Stewart Island southern tokoeka to forage on beaches in seaweed for sandhoppers. It also probes in the sand for other sand-dwelling invertebrates at night and sometimes during the day.

The range of the southern tokoeka has declined greatly. Today the population is about 6000 birds in the Fiordland area and 20,000 birds on Stewart Island.

Haast tokoeka
Apteryx australis 'Haast'

The Haast tokoeka is identified as a distinct form and is most closely related to the southern tokoeka. The average weight of an adult female is 3 kg and 2.5 kg for an adult male. They are about 40 cm in height, making them a similar size to the North Island brown kiwi. They have a very distinctive downward-curved bill.

The Haast tokoeka has a reddish-brown plumage. Its plumage is shaggy and hair-like and is harsh to the touch.

This kiwi is found from lowland forests to the high alpine tussock in South Westland. Their numbers are greater in the high subalpine to alpine areas, where they have large territories. Their nests and burrows are covered in snow during the winter months.

There are up to 250 individuals that are safer at higher altitudes where stoats are fewer. Research is being undertaken about their breeding habits and what threatens their survival in order to develop a management plan for their long-term conservation.

Male Haast tokoeka.

Female Haast tokoeka.

Little spotted kiwi
Apteryx owenii

This is the smallest of the kiwi species. The average weight of an adult female is 1.35 kg and an adult male is 1.15 kg. The little spotted kiwi's plumage is a pale grey mottled with white bars running across its feathers. This is what gives it a spotted appearance. Little spotted kiwi lay one egg that is incubated solely by the male. Juveniles reach adult size at 18 months of age.

The average length of this kiwi's bill when it is straight is 85 mm and when it is curved is 68 mm. Females have longer and more curved bills than males. Compared to other kiwi species the little spotted kiwi has a very long bill that is about 20 percent of its body length.

Fossil records indicate that little spotted kiwi were once widespread throughout New Zealand. In the North Island they are thought to have been virtually extinct before European arrival as only one live specimen was ever recorded. They existed in the South Island in abundant numbers but they eventually disappeared after the introduction of stoats during the 1880s.

In 1987 the last spotted kiwi living on D'Urville Island was removed and put onto Long Island in the Marlborough Sounds with two from Kapiti Island.

Today the biggest population of little spotted kiwi is found on Kapiti Island. It is unclear if they were naturally occurring there during pre-European times or if they were introduced to the island. The population is endangered but is breeding. Their future is brighter since the removal of rats and possums from the island.

Attempts have been made to establish new populations of little spotted kiwi on other islands including Red Mercury Island and the Hen and Chickens group of islands off the coast near Whangarei in Northland. More recently little spotted kiwi have been transferred from Kapiti Island to the Karori Wildlife Sanctuary in Wellington.

Great spotted kiwi
Apteryx haastii

The average weight of an adult female great spotted kiwi is 3.3 kg and an adult male is 2.4 kg. The average length of a female's bill is 120 mm and the male's is 97 mm. These birds have dark charcoal-grey plumage with lighter grey markings across their body. It is difficult to separate juvenile males and females until the female gains more weight and her bill gets characteristically longer.

Historically, the great spotted kiwi was probably was more widespread in the South Island than in the North Island, however fossils of great spotted kiwi bones are difficult to distinguish from those of the brown kiwi. Today, great spotted kiwi are found in a small area of northwest Nelson and in Westland, both in the South Island. They are equally at home in lowlands like the podocarp forests near Kahurangi Point or in highlands such as the tussock and beech forest areas of the Gouland Downs.

The great spotted kiwi is an endangered bird with a range that is shrinking.

HELPING THE KIWI SURVIVE

Kiwi survived for millions of years evolving alongside other birds that preyed on them. They had effective methods of protecting themselves but these methods were useless against the new mammalian predators.

In 1908, the New Zealand government passed a law banning the killing or capture of kiwi. In 1921 kiwi were declared to be absolutely protected. Despite these laws numbers have continued to decline. Today the total number of kiwi is estimated at around 50,000 birds. At the beginning of the 1900s there were thought to be 2.5 million kiwis in New Zealand.

The pressure from direct killing by humans for food and feathers probably caused the demise of little spotted kiwi in the North Island and their declining numbers in other areas. Early destruction of forests through fires first by early Maori, followed by European settlers' logging and burning activities, caused the kiwi's habitat and food supply to disappear. Nearly 80 percent of New Zealand's forests have been lost to exotic plantings and farmland.

The introduction of ground-dwelling predatory mammal species (for example stoats, dogs and cats) has also contributed greatly to the kiwi's demise. One report states that in Northland a single dog killed more than 600 kiwi on one rampage. Other causes of death have been the poison bait and gin traps laid down to eradicate possums.

This kiwi had been caught in a possum trap.

 31

Together, these factors have contributed to the numbers of kiwi rapidly declining. However, efforts are being made to conserve kiwi, including Kiwi Recovery Plans run by the Department of Conservation. Additionally, areas where kiwi live have and are being designated as kiwi reserves. Ecological services on mainland New Zealand manage and eradicate predators in these areas, which increases the kiwi's chances of survival (as well as that of other endangered species).

In the wild, kiwi chicks have only a 1 in 20 chance of reaching adulthood because of predators. Ninety-five percent of chicks are killed within the first month of their lives by introduced mammalian predators such as stoats. Many eggs don't hatch at all because of predator activity or natural accidents such as floods or burrow collapse. One of the programmes established to improve these odds is Operation Nest Egg.

Operation Nest Egg

Operation Nest Egg is an effort to help New Zealand's kiwi population survive. It involves carefully removing eggs from nests and artificially incubating them in conditions that resemble their wild habitat.

Specially trained 'kiwi dogs' are used to collect eggs from kiwi burrows. At a captive incubation centre, the egg is weighed. A fresh kiwi egg weighs between 400 and 450 grams and loses 12 to 16 percent of this weight during the incubation period to hatching. The eggs are then kept in a humidity-controlled incubator at about 37 degrees Celsius (this is about the same temperature that kiwi naturally incubate at) and are turned every day. This stops the developing embryo from sticking to the wall of its egg shell.

It takes a shorter time for eggs that are artificially incubated to hatch. This is because they are not subject to the variable temperature conditions in the wild so the embryos grow consistently every day.

After hatching and at about five days old, the chick is moved into a 'brooder'. The brooder contains moist soil, leaf litter and an artificial burrow. A diet consisting of a minced mixture of ox heart, rolled oats, vegetables, oil and vitamins and minerals is fed to the chicks. Included in the mix are worms, which provide the natural bacteria and grit to aid digestion that the chicks would normally pick up in the wild.

At seven days old the chicks naturally begin to forage. They are kept in captivity until they are about a month old. They are then big and strong enough to take care of themselves and are released into their natural habitat.

This southern tokoeka was killed by a stray dog.